Look What I Made!

Christina Goodings

LION
Children's Books

Text and artefacts by Christina Goodings
Photography by John Williams Studios, Thame
This edition copyright © 2001 Lion Publishing

The moral rights of the author
have been asserted

Published by
Lion Publishing plc
Sandy Lane West, Oxford, England
www.lion-publishing.co.uk
ISBN 0 7459 4473 6

First edition 2001
1 3 5 7 9 10 8 6 4 2 0

A catalogue record for this book is available
from the British Library

Typeset in Kidprint
Printed and bound in Singapore

Contents

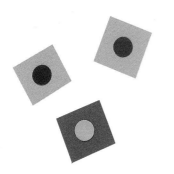

1 Calendar

Think about one special month of the year. Think of the colours you see: in the sky, in the weather, in the trees and in the flowers. Every month is lovely, every month is different.

Here is an idea for April.

You will need

- ☐ 20 cm x 20 cm plain square of interfacing
- ☐ scraps of fabric
- ☐ ribbons and trims
- ☐ scissors
- ☐ PVA glue
- ☐ brush
- ☐ strip of card 20 cm x 4 cm, with hanging hole punched
- ☐ stapler

1 Take a plain square. Choose fabric scraps, ribbons and trims to suit the month. Ask a grown-up to help you cut them to fit.

2 Brush glue on the wrong side of your fabrics, ribbons and trims. Stick them on the square. Leave the glue for a long time to dry.

3 Ask a grown-up to help staple a strip of card to the top of your square so it will be easy to hang up. ✋

✋ Note to grown-ups: The card strip helps the square to hang properly. Attach a hanging loop through the hole.

2 All the months

Make a patch for every month of the year.
(Look at the patch you made on page 1.)
Learn the names of the months.

January

February

March

April

May

June

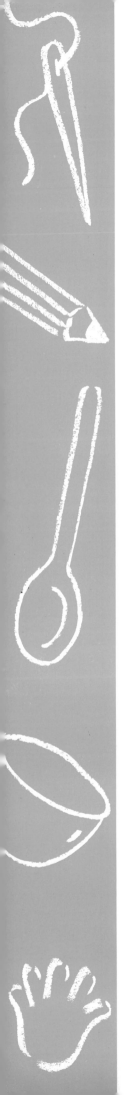

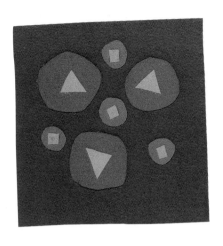

July

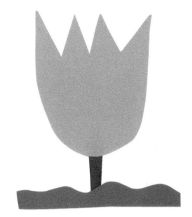

August

October

September

November

December

3 All the days

A real calendar has a chart showing all the days. Make a chart for each month of your calendar.

You will need

- [ ] 20 cm x 20 cm square of coloured paper to match each month
- [ ] copy of the chart, about 16 cm x 16 cm ✋
- [ ] coloured crayons
- [ ] scissors
- [ ] glue
- [ ] brush
- [ ] masking tape

1 Cut out the chart. Write on it the name of the month. Ask a grown-up to help you start writing numbers in the squares for each day of the month. Draw a star in any blank square.

2 Glue the chart on the coloured background.

3 Use masking tape on the wrong side to attach the chart to the calendar square.

Note to grown-ups: Copy the grid shown here. To help beginner writers, add dotted outlines for the name of each month and the numbers. If you are working with a group of children, you can then photocopy as many as you need for each month.

4 Winter snowman

Pure white snow is lovely and so much fun.
Enjoy winter... and then go indoors to get warm!

Tie a ribbon round your snowman's neck
as a scarf, and add a pipe-cleaner band
round the hat if you wish.

You will need

- [ ] curvy plastic bottle and bottle top
- [ ] PVA glue
- [ ] black paint mixed with PVA glue
- [ ] brushes
- [ ] quilt batting or cotton wool cut to wrap round the bottle
- [ ] string
- [ ] black felt
- [ ] scissors
- [ ] rubber bands
- [ ] twigs or black pipe cleaners
- [ ] ribbons

1 Paint the bottle top black and let the paint dry.

2 Practise wrapping the bottle in the batting. Then brush glue all over the bottle.

3 Roll the batting so it covers all the bottle. Wind string gently around to hold the batting close to the bottle as the glue dries. Then take the string off.

4 Cut a circle of black felt big enough for the hat brim. Ask a grown-up to help you snip the centre so you can fit it on the bottle opening. Add the bottle top as a cap.

5 Cut tiny pieces of black felt to be the eyes and mouth. Glue them in place.

6 Put a rubber band in place to mark the neck. If you wish, push pipe cleaners or twigs in place under the band for the arms.

5 Valentine hearts

Make a card for someone you love! Give them the card for Valentine's Day on 14 February.

You will need

- [ ] colour magazines and catalogues
- [ ] white paper with heart outline
- [ ] glue
- [ ] brush
- [ ] scissors
- [ ] blank, folded card (bigger than the heart!)

1 Choose who you are making a card for. Think of something they love, such as flowers. Snip tiny pictures and little bits of pictures of that thing from magazines.

2 Glue your cut-out pieces onto the heart. Overlap them so they make an all over design.

3 Ask a grown-up to help cut out the heart shape and stick it onto the card.

4 Write inside: I LOVE YOU!

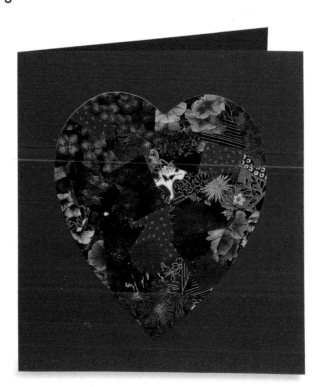

 Note to grown-ups: Use the heart template at the back of the book. If you plan to make lots of hearts, draw the outline once and photocopy it. Children can glue directly onto the copy. You can see enough of the outline on the other side to help you cut it out.

6 Pancakes

Make mini pancakes for the Pancake Day feast... some to eat, and some for traditional pancake games!

After Pancake Day, there are nearly seven weeks to Easter. Christians call this time Lent. The tradition is to live simply – no more pancakes!

Wash your hands before you begin any cooking, and put on an apron.

You will need

- ☐ 250 g self-raising flour
- ☐ 75 g caster sugar
- ☐ 2 tablespoons oil
- ☐ 2 tablespoons golden syrup
- ☐ 2 eggs
- ☐ 400 ml milk, plus a little more
- ☐ bowl
- ☐ whisk
- ☐ frying pan
- ☐ extra oil
- ☐ tablespoon
- ☐ spatula
- ☐ heatproof mat
- ☐ maple syrup, jam, lemon, sugar...

Try tossing cooked pancakes, using an unbreakable plate as a pan! Who can toss the best? The fastest? While running?

1 Put the flour and sugar in a bowl. Pour the oil, syrup and eggs into the middle. Whisk for a count of five.

2 Add the milk, splash by splash. After each splash, whisk for a count of five. Whisk in all 400 ml. The mixture should be like thick cream. If it is too thick, add a little more milk.

3 Ask a grown-up to wipe the frying pan with oil and heat it. Ask them to lift the pan onto the heatproof mat so you can add a spoonful of mix.

4 Watch as the grown-up cooks the pancake and the bubbles begin to burst. Then ask to have the pan on the heatproof mat so you can use the spatula to flip the pancake. Make lots. Eat pancakes with syrup, jam, lemon and sugar or maple syrup.

7 For Mummy!

One Sunday in Lent is a special day for mums. Think of all the good things mums do. Make a gift for your special mum.

You will need

- [ ] sponge
- [ ] paints
- [ ] rectangle of paper big enough to wrap neatly round a jar
- [ ] metallic pastels or crayons
- [ ] sticky tape
- [ ] jar
- [ ] flowers!

1 Dip the sponge in paint so it is just wet. Dab the sponge onto the paper to leave a speckly mark. Dip and dab to cover all your paper. Let the paint dry.

2 Use metallic pastels to draw pretty patterns on your paper.

3 Wrap the paper round the jar and tape it in place.

Arrange flowers in the vase to make a pretty gift.

8 Easter basket

Easter is a happy celebration, full of the joy of spring and new life. It is a time when Christians remember Jesus, who promised new life to all his followers.

Make a basket as bright as the flowers, as bright as the spring sunshine.

You will need

- ☐ paper plate, cut a bit like a flower and with holes punched ✋
- ☐ paint mixed with PVA glue
- ☐ brush
- ☐ ribbon or wool
- ☐ doily or circle of tissue paper

✋ Notes to grown-ups: Cut the plate using the plate template at the back of the book. Punch holes as marked.

Wrap a little sticky tape tightly round the end of the ribbon or wool to give it an 'end' like a shoelace so it is easy to thread. Snip it off when the threading is done.

1 Turn the plate-like-a-flower the wrong side up and paint it in Easter colours. Leave to dry.

2 Thread the ribbon in and out of the holes. Pull it through gently so it pulls the petals together and has two long ends.

3 Ask a grown-up to help you tie the ends into a bow. Now fill the basket with tissue paper so it is ready to hold an Easter gift.

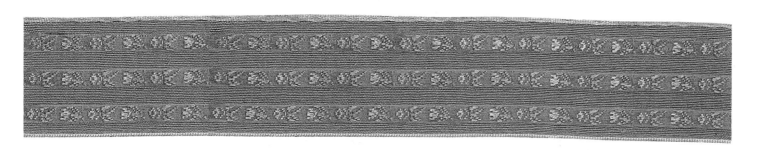

9 Easter cookies

These cookies make a lovely gift to put in your Easter basket. Everyone will enjoy eating them!

Wash your hands before you begin any cooking, and put on an apron.

You will need

- [ ] 150 g self-raising flour
- [ ] 1 teaspoon baking soda
- [ ] 1 teaspoon ginger
- [ ] 1 pinch cloves
- [ ] 50 g caster sugar
- [ ] 25 g brown sugar
- [ ] 75 g margarine or butter
- [ ] 2 tablespoons golden syrup
- [ ] bowl
- [ ] fork
- [ ] spatula
- [ ] baking tray lined with baking parchment
- [ ] heatproof mat
- [ ] wire rack

Ask a grown-up to preheat the oven to 160°C or Gas Mark 3.

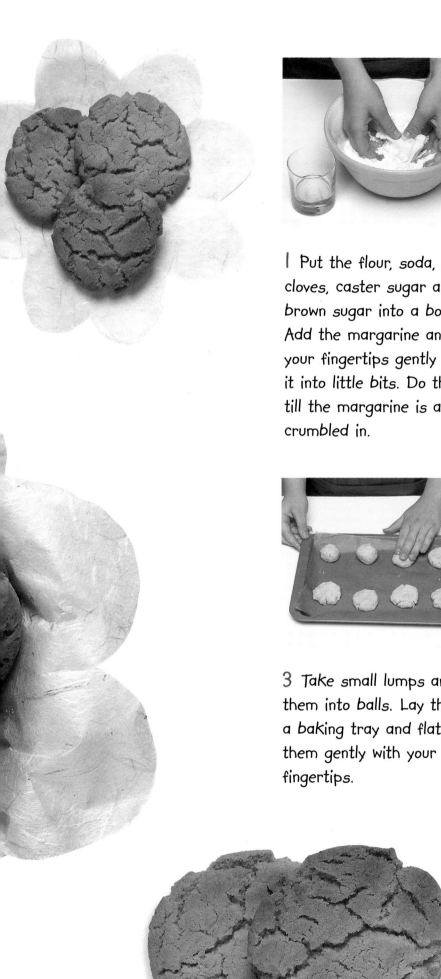

1 Put the flour, soda, ginger, cloves, caster sugar and brown sugar into a bowl. Add the margarine and with your fingertips gently break it into little bits. Do this till the margarine is all crumbled in.

2 Add the syrup and use a fork to mix everything into one soft ball.

3 Take small lumps and roll them into balls. Lay them on a baking tray and flatten them gently with your fingertips.

4 Ask a grown-up to bake the cookies for 8-10 minutes or until just turning brown. Have them lifted out of the oven and left on a heatproof mat to cool. After 15 minutes, lift the cookies onto the wire rack to finish cooling.

10 Sowing seeds

Sow seeds in spring. Watch your plant grow in the sun and the rain.

You will need

- [ ] large plastic bottle with the top cut off and a slit in the bottom
- [ ] water jug
- [ ] seed compost
- [ ] courgette seeds
- [ ] saucer
- [ ] garden pots and soil

1 Nearly fill the lower part of your bottle with seed compost. Place it on the saucer and water well.

2 Put three seeds in the seed compost a fingertip deep.

3 Wedge the top on the bottom part of the bottle. Place the whole thing on a windowsill and wait for seedlings to grow.

4 When the seedlings have 4–6 leaves, carefully take them out of the little pot and replant them in a big pot of soil or in the ground. Place them in the open where they will get a lot of sun and rain. If they start to look dry, water them.

Your plants will soon grow bigger. Watch yellow flowers unfold. Some of them have *baby courgettes* behind them. When the flowers fall, the green courgettes start to grow.

Note to grown-ups: The flowers without courgettes behind are male flowers. To make sure that the female flowers are fertilized, take a male flower, strip off the petals, and push the pollen inside the female flowers.

11 Holiday frame

Summer is a good time for going on holiday.
Here is a frame for a holiday picture, to help you
remember the fun you had.

You will need

- [ ] gesso
- [ ] pasta shells
- [ ] brushes
- [ ] piece of cardboard cut into a frame about 5 cm wide
- [ ] paints in two colours of sandy yellow
- [ ] glue
- [ ] masking tape
- [ ] photo or picture

1 First paint the pasta shells with gesso. The first coat will dry quickly. Give the shells a second coat.

2 Paint the frame. Keep the two colours separate, but keep dipping your brush first into one and then the other. Swirl the colours together on the frame. Let the paint dry.

3 Dab the frame colours onto the shells to look like a dusting of sand.

4 Glue the shells in place on the frame.

5 Use masking tape on the back to hold your holiday picture in place.

12 Harvest muffins

The courgettes you grew are vegetables (see page 10). People eat courgettes steamed or fried along with their potatoes and peas. You can also use your harvest courgettes to make muffins!

Wash your hands before you begin any cooking, and put on an apron.

You will need

- ☐ 2 small courgettes (or 1 larger one)
- ☐ 2 eggs
- ☐ 175 g caster sugar
- ☐ 150 ml sunflower oil
- ☐ 2 teaspoons vanilla
- ☐ 250 g self-raising flour
- ☐ 1 teaspoon baking soda
- ☐ 1 teaspoon salt
- ☐ 1 teaspoon cinnamon
- ☐ 1/2 teaspoon nutmeg
- ☐ 50 g chopped walnuts (optional)
- ☐ grater and plate
- ☐ fork
- ☐ 2 bowls
- ☐ spoon
- ☐ muffin cases in a muffin tray
- ☐ heatproof mat
- ☐ wire rack

Ask a grown-up to preheat the oven to 160°C or Gas Mark 3.

1 Grate the courgettes onto the plate.

2 Put the eggs, sugar, oil and vanilla into one bowl and stir with the fork to mix everything up.

3 Put the flour, soda, salt, cinnamon and nutmeg into the other bowl. Tip in the egg mix and stir together.

4 Add the grated courgette mix (and the walnuts if you are using them) and stir again.

5 Put a spoonful of mix in each muffin case. Fill each case a bit more than half full.

6 Ask a grown-up to put the muffins in the oven to bake for about 12 minutes. The muffins are done when the top feels just firm. Let the muffins cool on a heatproof mat for 15 minutes, then lift them onto a rack to finish cooling.

13 Autumn trees

Watch the trees change colour in autumn! Try to find leaves of every colour: red, brown, orange and yellow.

You will need

- ☐ card shapes like lollipop trees ✋
- ☐ wool and yarn in autumn colours
- ☐ scissors
- ☐ sticky tape

1 Take a lollipop tree. On the wrong side, tape a piece of red wool in place. Wind it through one of the snips. Wind the wool to a snip on the opposite edge, and then round the back to another snip.

2 Keep winding in the same way till the tree is crisscrossed with wool. Cut the wool and tape the end on the back.

3 Do the same again with another colour. You can choose wispy white to look like frost.

4 Fold back the two tabs at the base of the trunk so your tree will stand up. Tape the tabs together.

✋ Note to grown-ups: The tree template is at the back of the book. Some children may be able to help cut the tree shape.

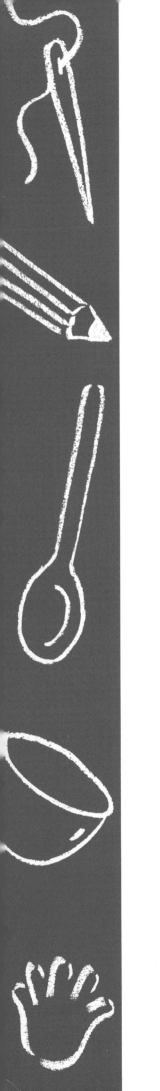

14 Dark nights and scary shadows

By the end of October, the nights are long. Night-time shadows can be scary! Make a dark woodland place where SPIDERS lurk. Remember always that, however dark and scary a place may be, the light will come again.

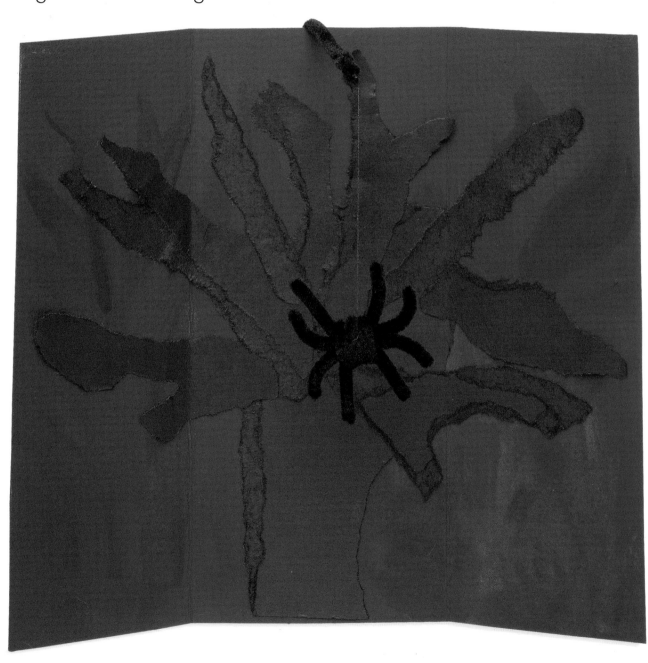

You will need

- [ ] rectangle of card, about 25 cm high and 40 cm wide
- [ ] paint in night-time colours
- [ ] brushes
- [ ] thin black card
- [ ] glue
- [ ] black pipe cleaners: four bits that are 5 cm long and two that are 10 cm long
- [ ] sticky tape
- [ ] thread

1 Fold the card as shown. Then paint the outside of the flaps and all of the inside in night-time colours, with swirling shadow shapes. Let the paint dry.

2 Tear the black card to make a thick tree trunk shape and oddly shaped branches.

3 Arrange them on the card to look like a tree, then glue them in place.

4 Make the spider: hold the four short bits of pipe cleaner together and wind one longer bit round the middle of them. Arrange the short bits on each side to look like legs!

5 Wind one end of a thread around the spider so it dangles. Wind the other end around the last bit of pipe cleaner. Tape the pipe cleaner to the back of your card.

15 Advent gifts

Count the days in December that lead to Christmas. This time is the season of Advent, when Christians look forward to remembering the birth of Jesus. Here are 25 presents, one for each day of December, all the way to Christmas!

Unwrap one gift every day in December.

You will need

- [ ] small tree in a pot (twigs in soil, or a tiny evergreen)
- [ ] strong cartridge paper
- [ ] paint mixed with PVA glue
- [ ] brush
- [ ] chocolate buttons
- [ ] Kitchen foil
- [ ] pipe cleaners
- [ ] ruler, pencil and scissors

1 Take a piece of cartridge paper. Scrumple it carefully, then smooth it. Do this two or three times to make it crinkly all over.

2 Paint the paper with the paint and glue. Let it dry, then paint the other side.

3 While the paint dries, wrap 25 chocolate buttons in small pieces of Kitchen foil.

4 Ask a grown-up to help you mark the painted paper into 10 cm squares. Cut them out.

5 Put a foil-wrapped chocolate button in the middle of a square and fold the corners in.

6 Hold each little parcel with a pipe cleaner.

Note to grown ups: If you wish, you can add a numbered sticky label to each gift to help you keep track!

16 Advent tree

Unwrap a gift each day through the days of December, the days of Advent. Twist the wrapping on the tree. By Christmas time, you will have your own decorated tree. Happy Christmas – Jesus is born! Joy to all the world!

You will need

☐ Advent tree and gifts (see page 15)

1 Each day, take the paper from a mini parcel and smooth it. Then zig-zag fold it.

2 Take the pipe cleaner and wrap it round the middle of the paper.

3 Use the ends of the pipe cleaner to attach the paper to the tree. Fan out the ends of the paper.

17 Christmas gifts

Christmas is a time for loving and sharing.
Make giant truffles to give as gifts.

Wash your hands before you begin any cooking, and put on an apron.

You will need

- ☐ 100 g butter
- ☐ 200 g chocolate chips
- ☐ 100 g trifle sponges
- ☐ 100 g ground almonds
- ☐ 100 g icing sugar
- ☐ 3 egg yolks

- ☐ 1 teaspoon vanilla
- ☐ 2 bowls: 1 large, 1 small
- ☐ fork
- ☐ plate
- ☐ paper cases
- ☐ spoon

1 Put the butter and chocolate into the small bowl. Ask a grown-up to help you microwave them till they melt. Stir.

2 Crumble the trifle sponges into the large bowl, with the ground almonds and icing sugar. Mix.

3 Add the egg yolks and the vanilla and mix.

4 Pour the melted butter and chocolate into the mixture in the big bowl.

5 Stir everything together. Then put the mixture in the fridge to chill till it is firm.

6 Take the mixture out of the fridge. Roll spoonfuls into balls. Put each ball in a paper case. Keep the truffles chilled till you are ready to eat them.

18 Gift wrap

Here is a lovely way to wrap your truffles.
It is a good way to wrap any small gift!

You will need

- [ ] squares of kitchen foil
- [ ] squares of net in different colours,
  each 50 cm x 50 cm
- [ ] twist ties or pipe cleaners
- [ ] curling ribbon
- [ ] plant label or similar

1 Wrap the truffle or small gift in foil to hide it.

2 Ask a grown-up to cut squares of net big enough to wrap the gift with enough spare to make a big ruffle. Choose three squares for each gift. Arrange them as shown so the corners stick out in a star shape.

3 Lay the gift on top in the middle. Gather the net in your hands and tie it close to the gift with a twist tie or pipe cleaner.

4 Add lots of ribbon. Ask a grown up to help with the knots. Curl the ribbon by pulling a plastic plant label along the underside really fast.

Christmas cards

Send a Christmas message to those you love!

You will need

- ☐ card shapes ✋
- ☐ coloured paper
- ☐ scissors
- ☐ coloured stickers
- ☐ star stickers
- ☐ glue
- ☐ brush
- ☐ sticky tape
- ☐ small pieces of
   twist tie or pipe cleaners

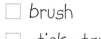

1 Cut the coloured paper into strips and cut the strips into squares.

2 Decorate each square with a sticker.

3 Glue the shapes on the front of the tree card.

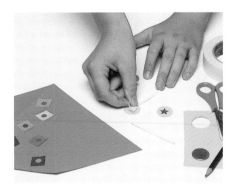

4 Now cut a circle for the top of your card and decorate it with a star sticker. Tape the circle onto a pipe cleaner.

5 Tape the pipe cleaner end of the circle at the point of the card on the wrong side so the circle sticks out on the top.

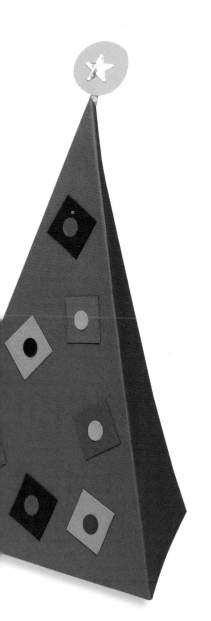

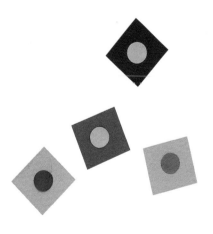

🖐 Note to grown-ups: The card template is at the back of the book. Cut the shape, score the fold lines and fold accurately to help give a good finish.

6 Write inside: HAPPY CHRISTMAS!

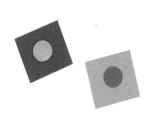

Christmas stars

The story of Jesus tells of a bright star shining over the place where he was born. Make sparkly stars to hang everywhere... on the Christmas tree, hanging from long strings or attached to paper chains.

You will need

- ☐ circle of card with 5 holes punched and numbered exactly as shown 🖐
- ☐ Christmassy yarn
- ☐ pipe cleaners
- ☐ sticky tape

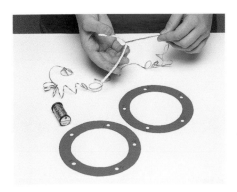  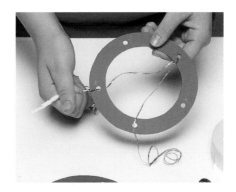

1 Cut 1.80 m yarn. Fold a pipe cleaner around one end of the yarn and twist the ends of it to make a 'needle'.

2 Thread the yarn up through hole 1. Leave a long tail dangling (about 30 cm) and tape the yarn on the wrong side behind hole 1 so it will not slip.

3 Now take the yarn down through hole 2 and up through hole 3.

 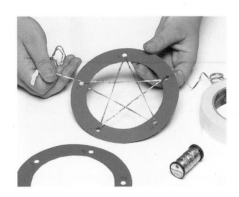 

4 Now take it down through hole 4, up through hole 5...

5 ...AND down through hole 1, up through hole 2, down through hole 3...

6 ...Up through hole 4, down through hole 5 AND up through hole 1.

7 Now ask a grown-up to help you tie the dangly tail from the beginning and the last bit of thread at the end in a knot that sits just on the edge of the card. Use the ends to hang the star.

Note to grown-ups: The card template is at the back of the book.

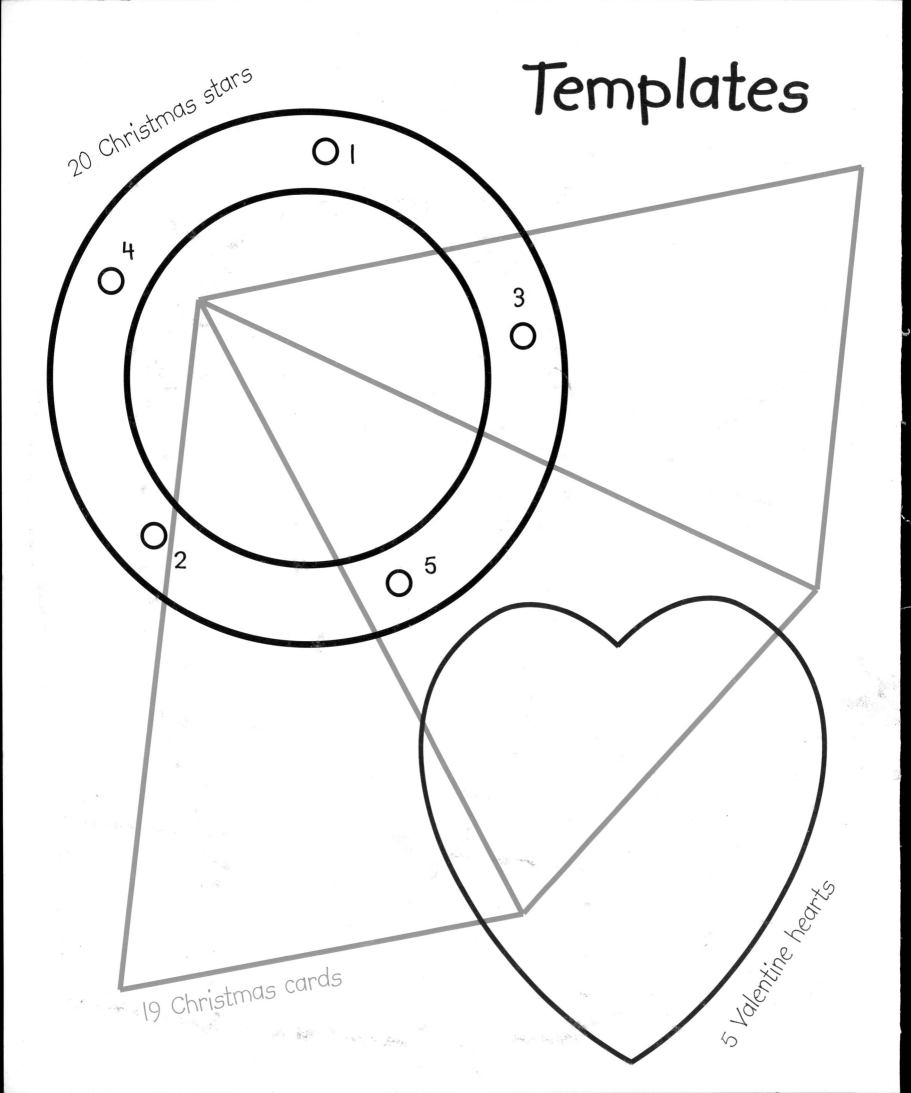

Templates

20 Christmas stars

O 1

O 4

3 O

O 2

O 5

19 Christmas cards

5 Valentine hearts